AUSTRALIA

The Editorial Committee is most grateful to all those who have so kindly helped in the selection of illustrations, especially to officials of the various public Museums, Libraries and Galleries, and to all others who have generously allowed pictures and MSS. to be reproduced.

AUSTRALIA

ARNOLD HASKELL

With
twelve plates in colour
and twenty-three illustrations in
black and white

Published for
PENNS IN THE ROCKS PRESS
by
WILLIAM COLLINS OF LONDON
1941

PRODUCED BY ADPRINT LONDON

PRINTED IN GREAT BRITAIN

LIST OF ILLUSTRATIONS

PLATES IN COLOUR

BLACK AND WHITE ILLUSTRATIONS

BRIEF HISTORICAL CHRONOLOGY

1642   Tasman discovers Van Diemen's Land.

1770   Captain Cook lands in Botany Bay.

1778   Foundation of the Colony of New South Wales.

1791   First land grant in Australia.

1793   Arrival of first free settlers.

1796   John MacArthur introduces the Merino sheep.

1797   Coal discovered in Newcastle, N.S.W.

1804   Lieut.-Gen. Collins lands at Risdon Cove, Van Diemen's Land, after an abortive attempt to settle what became Victoria.

1813   Discovery of a route across the Blue Mountains.

1825   Van Diemen's Land proclaimed a colony (name changed to Tasmania in 1856).

1826   Official proclamation of settlement at Brisbane.

1829   Foundation of Western Australia. Sturt discovers Darling River.

1830   Sturt reaches the mouth of the Murray.

1834   The Hentys land at Portland.

1835   John Batman signs treaty with aborigines at Port Phillip.
Fawkner arrives at Port Phillip.

1836   South Australia proclaimed a colony. Mitchell discovers *Australia Felix.*

1840   Transportation to N.S.W. ceases.

1851   Gold discovered in Victoria. Victoria proclaimed a colony.

1852   First mail steamer, P. & O. *Chusan,* arrives in Sydney.

1859   Queensland proclaimed a colony.

1860   McDonald Stuart reaches the centre of Australia.

1861   First Melbourne Cup run. First English cricket team visits Australia.

1868   Transportation to Western Australia ceases.

1869   Opening of Suez Canal brings Australia nearer home.

1884   First cargo of frozen meat reaches London from Brisbane.

1885   First shipment of Queensland sugar arrives.

1901   Federation of the colonies.

1914   Australia at war with Germany.

1939   Australia at war with Germany.

INTRODUCTION

" AUSTRALIA, MY SECOND COUNTRY "

BEFORE landing on the vast continent of Australia it is essential to inspect the credentials of the writer through whose eyes it will be seen. My first visit to Australia took place by chance, four years ago. I was bored at the prospect and unwilling but I fell in love with Australia before I had been there many hours and from that moment I resolved to see as much of the country as I could, to meet as many of its people in all walks of life, to study its history, read its poetry, see its painting, enjoy its food and wines.

I spent a first seven months in Australia, returned home and read up my subject, making the collection of early *Australiana* an absorbing hobby. I then went out again. I had rationalised my love and with knowledge it grew.

On my return, I wrote *Waltzing Matilda*, a very personal account of those travels—it gives me more pleasure to re-read than anything I have written. Such then are my qualifications ; enthusiasm backed up by a certain amount of hard study. An Australian might certainly have presented a more intimate study, but there is much at which he could no longer wonder, and wonder is the very essence of enjoyable travel.

Also, a national might easily be biassed by some sectional feeling. I say this because certain writers in Australia have said : He is very devoted to us, *tant mieux*, but he is misguided. He has met the wrong people (*i.e.*, not our particular set) ; he is superficial (*i.e.*, has not written a blue book) ; should have taken D. H. Lawrence to heart, etc.

I make these remarks in no spirit of resentment, but to show the nature of the task a travel commentator undertakes and to underline once again my intention, which is *to make people think for themselves*. This is a book of hints.

I cannot pretend to tell Australians themselves anything new about their own country, except this—how it strikes a European. Therefore I make no apology for writing on so vast a subject as Australia, " my second country."

ARNOLD HASKELL

Bournemouth, *May*, 1940

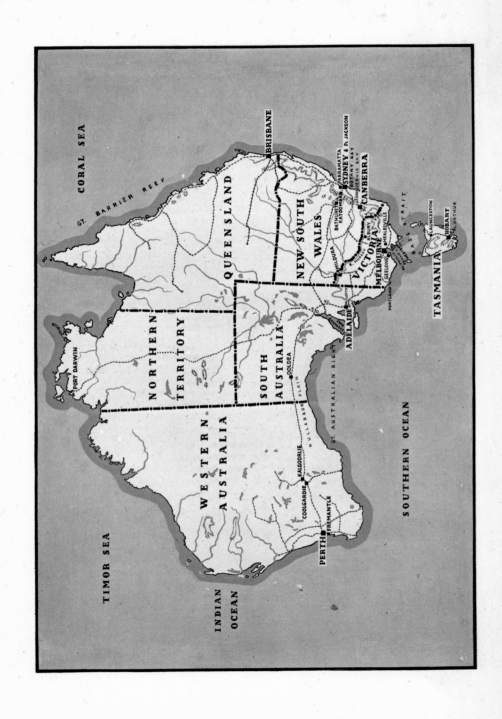

WESTERN AUSTRALIA

THE whole history of Australia is bound up with ocean travel, and it is best to reach it by sea, for its isolation accounts for many of the things that we shall notice. The early settlers reached it after many months of hardship and, as the shipping records show, of danger. To-day we are spoilt and grumble if the ship's band does not provide the latest tunes.

To the visitor, the first impression of Australia will be coloured by this long, lazy voyage, punctuated by the many exotic ports of call that flash past him with the rapidity of a film travelogue and that seem equally detached from reality. The whole of India becomes a dish of curry and a snake-charmer ; the Pacific the surf at Waikiki. If he comes from Europe, his first Australian port will be Fremantle, Western Australia. His very first feeling will certainly be one of disappointment. " I have sailed half-way around the world. The last time I set foot on land was in Ceylon. What life, colour, glamour, and now I seem to be back in England and not such an attractive part of England at that." Such is the impression by the customs' sheds, half an hour after the tedious routine of medical inspection, when a bored doctor meets a weary, bad-tempered passenger.

Fremantle is a port like any other port and the details of its busy life are all the more stark for being seen against the sunshine instead of through the softening mists of Tilbury or Liverpool. If the tourist goes on shore, the unfavourable impression will be still further strengthened by the warehouses, factories, hoardings, cinemas, pubs and small villas that line this roadway as they do his own. The dock-workers look very much like British dock-workers and use very much the same language, stronger if anything. The Australian is a master of oaths.

Later, much later, he will find out that, in spite of the marked resemblance with home, the differences are fully as marked. He is still too much under the influence of tourist-leaflet exoticism, to show any interest in such a busy port as Fremantle and the lives of its peaceful industrious inhabitants.

The second impression follows rapidly, even dramatically on the first. " Half an hour ago we were at home, but here are plants by the score that I never knew existed, fantastic trees and bushes, a fierce blaze of colour."

This change from drab to beautiful has come about in half an hour's car ride from Fremantle to the King's Park, Perth. Spring is the time to see this marvel when the ground is alive with wild flowers, extraordinary in form, unusual in colour, the red gum-trees ablaze with their blossom. This is the Australian bush, tamed it is true, but fantastic enough to make us believe at last in everyone of those 12,000 miles, the pin holes on the smoking-room chart.

The first time that the word Australia assumes a true meaning for the traveller is here. It may fascinate or repel, it will surely mystify, it cannot leave the beholder indifferent. It has none of the green serenity of our own countryside, none of the suggestion that it has befriended man. Neither has it the humid vine-tangled impenetrability of the tropical jungle. It is a thing entirely apart, an extraordinary combination of the most vivid and the most subtle colouring ; fierce reds, yellows, purples with every gradation of brown, black and grey, from charcoal to the silver of the etcher's pencil. The bush is dominated by the gum-tree—straggly, gnarled, its bark peeling and hanging in tatters, its bole often hollowed and cracked, the tender shoots alone revealing that there is sap and life. Everywhere we shall see the gum, either as a dried-up, drought-stricken dwarf or a towering forest giant.

We pause here before visiting the city and are reminded of the antiquity of Australia as an independent continent. That is the background against which we shall view the latest efforts of man to build a home and a civilisation of his own. Out of the bush man builds his cities, struggles for his wealth, finds many of the things that have turned the Englishman of yesterday into the Australian of to-day. It has given a theme to the poets, colour and form to the painters.

ON FEELING A FOREIGNER : A TRAVEL ATTITUDE

The first Australian monument to be seen, and, like King's Park, it explains many things, is the University of Western Australia, a magnificent building and a symbol. The architect has taken a European model, Italian renaissance, and with rare tact has adapted it to the Australian scene. In his main hall he has used as decorative motives the designs of the primitive aboriginal artists, the first recognition of the high artistic value of this work. Already this modern building has an atmosphere ; it has taken root, belonging to the scene like the gum, the waratah and the wattle. And the University is a free one.

Such an institution would attract the excited attention of the " advanced " thinker were it situated in Russia, it would be considered the very last word in the ordered planning of a new world. And so it is, right here in Perth, W.A. But, as I have said, the average traveller has left his vision *en route* in some

IN THE FLINDERS RANGES
South Australia

faked native bazaar and the Western Australian himself is proud but has ceased to wonder. The Australian is in any case a bad booster. The only spirit in which to travel in Australia is in the same state of excited expectancy adopted by the tourist in Europe's much publicised experimental states, to see beyond and behind the suburbia of Fremantle which, incidentally, is not the suburbia of London. No continent contains more surprises and to the Englishman they are all carefully hidden by the atmosphere of home.

There is nothing the Englishman dislikes more than the feeling that he is a foreigner and, if he is not of an inquisitive frame of mind, he can travel right across Australia without that unwelcome feeling, but at the sacrifice of seeing nothing of an independent culture, the result of a new environment and a hundred and fifty years of separate history. As we travel from state to state, we shall understand that yesterday's colony is a nation and shall appreciate the nature of the links that bind that nation to the mother country. They are a constant source of inspiration at the present day.

From the King's Park we can see a miniature Perth down below, a white city nestling on the banks of the Swan River, so named by the Dutch discoverers. The black swan—and he still dwells in his river, side by side with the pelican, but no longer in his thousands—is the crest of Western Australia.

Every Australian capital has its characteristics clearly and well defined. Perth is a serene country town. Its core is a dignified and busy modern metropolis; surrounding that small core is a garden city of trim houses and small, colourful, well-kept gardens. It is evident that the metropolitan core

11

represents business and not gaiety and that the centre of pleasure and entertaining is the home. Perth has its theatre, but is starved of the good shows it would patronise and relies on the cinema or on its own amateurs.

This pleasant small town, and I use the term as one of praise, is the capital of the largest state in Australia, stretching from the Great Australian Bight into the near tropics of the Timor Sea, a wheat-growing, timber-producing, pearl-fishing and gold-bearing state.

Statistics can often be dramatic ; they are in the case of such a city. Western Australia has an area of 975,920 square miles, a population of 460,161, nearly 50 per cent. of whom live in Perth. These figures show that the city, like all Australian cities, is over-populated and they also suggest that Western Australia is still in its infancy. They reveal Australia's greatest problem, that of population. In this case statistics are grossly misleading. It is essential to know Australia in order to understand the problem.

Australia is greatly underpopulated, but nothing like to the extent that figures of areas and population show. Much of the land is at present uninhabitable—our first train journey will show that other sections are only suitable for grazing at certain periods, according to the rainfall. Emigration and the improvement of the land must go hand in hand and such improvement requires vast capital outlay. Coloured labour would create a far more serious problem by lowering the whole standard of living and imperilling Australian democracy.

Only a peacetime economy can solve the problem. Like many other problems its solution must be postponed. Meanwhile Australia's sacrifice in man power is very real.

EARLY DIFFICULTIES

This huge state is in a sense isolated from the life of the rest of Australia and many an Australian familiar with Bond Street and the Rue de la Paix has spent at most a few fleeting hours in Perth.

Her infancy was more troubled than that of the other colonies. Started in 1829, in a hurry to anticipate a possible French occupation, badly financed and over-publicised, the early settlers went through a period of intolerable privation. Luxurious furniture brought out from England in hopes of colonial ease lay rotting on the banks of the Swan, whilst its owners grubbed a bare existence or fled to the Eastern States. Incessant toil and the development of fertile land kept the colony alive, though in 1849 it had to petition to become a convict settlement. Not until 1885 did it come into its own with the sensational discovery of gold at the " Golden mile " at Kalgoorlie. To-day Western Australia is prosperous, but like Queensland one can still feel the atmosphere of pioneering more fully alive than in the other states, giving the Western Australian vigour, independence of thought and vitality, that is everywhere noticeable in his speech and bearing.

12

THE FIRST SITE OF ADELAIDE

From a print, c. 1837

TWO VIEWS OF MELBOURNE

From a print dedicated to Sir Henry Barkly, Governor of Victoria 1856-1863

SOUTH AUSTRALIA

THE NEW ANGLO-SAXONDOM

THE next city to visit is Adelaide, capital of South Australia. Its distance from Perth is the same as from London to Constantinople, a point worth remembering when you ask an Adelaide man if he knows Jones of Perth. Incidentally it is ten to one that he *does* know Jones of Perth. That is one of the characteristics of Australia ; its vast spaces and yet the possibility of maintaining what can only be described as a " clubable " atmosphere.

This will be the first and last hint of that lavish, touching hospitality. It is famous, but all too often monopolises any mention of Australia, giving the impression that the chief merit, nay the very *raison d'être* of the Australian is to entertain the visiting European. Which is all too easy, like the cocktail-party travel philosophy that sums up national characteristics in a slogan : La France l'amour, England sport, etc. People are too complex for labels and the Australian is as complex as any ; more so, for he is not always highly articulate, and certainly not given to discussing the Australian Soul. There is an Australian way of thinking and it will not be found through meeting a travelling Australian, but only gradually, there in Australia under the sun against the background of the Australian immensity.

What are the Australians ? That is far easier to answer. They are " the new Anglo-Saxondom," those men of spirit and enterprise who felt cramped at home. Some few were convicts, some younger sons, some men who would answer the call of adventure whether it came from the Klondyke, the Rand or Bendigo. They had to work hard or go under, have initiative or go under, they also had to lay aside some of the arts and graces of the old country. They lived in solitude, battled with natural conditions, covered vast distances. They were *always* wiser and more enterprising than the home government. Australia was founded in a fit of absence of mind, it required exceptional qualities in the men on the spot to make it succeed.

They conquered, prospered, or at any rate made a living, and then settled down to enjoy the land that had in two generations become their country. They had breathing space to look about them and to think. These were not people who were going to take things for granted. They were going to examine tradition, sift good from bad and use just what they wanted. At last they had sufficient leisure to find the need for artistic self-expression. *Australian democracy is the result of the most gigantic accidental experiment in history.*

13

It is possible to go to Adelaide by boat across a notorious stretch of water, the great Australian Bight, or by train.

The train itself is comfortable, but not luxurious in the American sense of the word. The route is remarkable, an explorer's journey across a mysterious desert, the Nullarbor Plain. First we pass the famous gold towns of Coolgardie and Kalgoorlie. To-day they are taken for granted, but only yesterday the value of their immense gold was problematical. There was no water. The building of the pipe-line was an epic of Western Australian history, for in this continent, where flocks have moved over the countryside as armies of occupation, such peaceful conquests are history. Then the train passes through a country of stunted and sickly trees and into the desert of the Nullarbor Plain, formerly a sea-bed, a part of the Bight. This is a desert, but in the Australian manner. It is starved of water, but a good year's rainfall will see it covered with flowers and feed. A desert can become a garden overnight, it can remain a garden for a year and feed its thousands of sheep, and then once again it becomes a desert. These plains over which we pass are not yet fully charted. To the north they are the home of the blackfellow, a paradise for anthropologist, geologist and naturalist. Ooldea, the last station before the plain, the last natural supply of water, was from time immemorial the meeting place of the aboriginal tribes. To-day some half-dozen miserable specimens struggle up to the train to beg tobacco and pennies. All they have left to mark their passing is a series of picturesque name-places.

On the burning ground there is a bright red flower, Sturt's desert pea, named after Charles Sturt, the father of Australian exploration, a particularly fitting memorial. On such a journey we can realise that in Australia the explorer has been the outstanding man and that the pioneer either followed close upon his heels or, without knowing it, was himself an explorer.

As the train puffs on we can see vast glistening lakes that hold out a promise of cool refreshment. They are salt, the water has evaporated or sunk into some vast underground sea. And the sun sets over these plains with a splendour that only Kansas can rival.

We pass two nights on this train, as cut off from the world as in a ship at sea. It is well to reach a city again.

LIGHT'S CITY

Adelaide is immediately friendly, cradled at the foot of a gentle range of hills named Lofty. It is a small city, but conceived on a large scale, so that to see the country at the foot of each street is something of a surprise. Colonel Light, its original planner, misunderstood during his lifetime, was a man of the future. Never can a city have had healthier lungs. There is about Adelaide an atmosphere of unostentatious prosperity and of a sense of values. Like

A SCENE AT HAWKESBURY AGRICULTURAL COLLEGE
New South Wales

KANGAROOS JUMPING BY A BOUNDARY FENCE
New South Wales

the Hague it is a big village, and it is content to be a big village.   Never have
I felt a more peaceful and harmonious atmosphere.

Adelaide has known no convict settlement and no gold rush.   Its original
settlers were men of substance, their interests pastoral.   In 1836 they set out
to found a state according to the ideal of Edward Gibbon Wakefield, the
purchase of land to subsidise the labour of free settlers.   In practice the scheme
did not work out and for the first years of their existence they suffered hardship
and privation.   But the land was good and so were the settlers.   It was about
them that the explorer Governor Grey coined the phrase " The new Anglo-
Saxondom."   But South Australia was also fortunate in its German settlers,
peaceful Moravians fleeing religious persecution in Germany.   Their influence
can be seen in many trim German villages around Adelaide and in the vineyards
that they cultivate.

The wine of Australia is known only to the rest of the world as a popular
commercial enterprise that sells a blend in the bulk.   South Australia alone
among the States is wine-drinking and its connoisseurs know that there are
good vintages that deserve better exploitation than they have received.   When
Australian wine drops its imitative phase and begins to develop Australian names
to describe Australian qualities it will find its way into the cellars of the dis-
criminating.   Its chance is coming with the plight of the European vineyards
on both sides of the Rhine.

As in Perth the centre of Adelaide life is the home.   There is little theatrical
activity, yet a large public eager for flesh and blood artists,.   The University
is beginning to take an interest in the theatre, and it is likely that, as in

America, the University will save the Australian theatre. In Adelaide the influence of the University can be felt.

The museum is exceptionally interesting, not only for its paintings, but for its large ethnographical collection.

There is an interesting and profitable source of study in the unhappy aboriginal as an artist. Already we have seen the fine use of aboriginal motives in the big hall of the Western Australian University. The French have shown the value of native art in their exploitation, sometimes over-commercialised, of the more sophisticated art of the Gabun. America too has recognised the value of primitive art. Australia as a whole is still unaware of its rich store-house of information and the majority of anthropologists have been studying the aboriginal purely from the point of view of social organisation and totemism. Whether the aboriginal artist decorated his weapons and utensils to satisfy an artistic craving is doubtful, though one cannot rule out the æsthetic impulse. His aim was doubtless to give them some secret power, but the fact remains that his drawings on bark and carvings in wood and rock are striking in pattern and colouring. The unfortunate black can still offer something of value to Australian culture, something that is Australia's alone. There in Adelaide is the material of a lifetime.

" ORSTRYLIAN "

There is another thing that is Australia's alone—you will have grown used to it by now—the great Australian accent, which is *not* Cockney. Its origin is a mystery. Here are the facts. It varies but slightly throughout the length and breadth of the continent, it bears no relation to position or culture. The original settlers came from all parts of the United Kingdom. Whence this particular and distinctive manner of speech ? " Pioneering," says an Australian friend. " Solitude makes a man slipshod and Australian speech calls for the smallest possible effort." That is but one theory. But without a doubt a hundred and fifty years have made a definitely recognisable speech that is not merely uncultivated English. It is not very pretty, but no worse than certain examples of B.B.C. English. It is the one thing that most people think they know about Australia, the Cockney, which is not Cockney at all, and the Australian has a right to be somewhat sensitive, not about the speech, but the superior references to it.

ESCAPE WITH A BILLY

Adelaide is a city of escape; every street leads into the country and the playgrounds of the city are the beautiful Mount Lofty ranges, green in spring-time and a mass of blossom. What a scene for a characteristic Australian picnic, the centre of which is the billy-can, a tin container that can either be bought at an elegant store or more often made out of that most useful piece of

Australian furniture, the kerosene tin. It is suspended over a fire of eucalypt twigs, pleasantly aromatic, and in it the strong tea boils and bubbles. It tastes like no other tea, I doubt if it tastes of tea at all, but it is a grand drink, magnificently quenching, and the billy is a symbol like the camp fire of other lands. The solid part of the picnic consists either of sausages, eucalypt-grilled, or of mutton chops cooked in their own fat on a grid that can be improvised from a few feet of fencing wire. Sandwiches have no real part in an Australian picnic. The Australian likes meat, as much of it as possible and as many times a day.

It is hot, not an enervating heat, but the heat of brilliance. The green of early spring is giving way to patches of brown and yellow, the birds are resting, but the cicada hums like the singing of a hundred wires. The picnicker relaxes, pleasantly dazed, and soon he is asleep.

When he awakes the sun is no longer overhead and he is surrounded by a new life. In the distance there is the tinkle of small bells, song of the bell bird, this is brusquely interrupted by a shrill chatter, as a flock of brightly winged parrots flashes past, rosellas or scarlet lowrys, drawing attention to their beauty by the dissonance of their screech. Small honey-eaters hover in and out of the shrubs and then, a sudden peal of hysterical laughter working itself into a climax, as the master-clown, the Kookaburra, feels the approach of night. There is no twilight, a sudden deepening of colour and all is dark. Then the stars descend till they almost touch the trees. The heat of the day has left a smell of aromatic gum on the air and the evening breeze rustles the leaves and the tangled dangling bark.

COLLINS STREET MELBOURNE
Victoria

VICTORIA

SOAMES IN MELBOURNE

IN many respects Melbourne is the most difficult of all the cities to describe, the most difficult to get to know. The usual travel descriptions are made by using the well-known rivalry between Melbourne and Sydney—I have been guilty of this myself—and saying that Melbourne is English and Sydney American. Unsatisfactory and untrue. Yet the difference in appearance and spirit is far greater than the easy night's journey by train would suggest ; it may be found in history.

Melbourne is a great capital city, solid and dignified. I have only to hear the name to think of civic fathers. It is a beautiful city with its main artery, Collins Street, one of the finest boulevards in the world. There is also a more intimate beauty, a picturesqueness that belongs to the old world and that makes it difficult for one to believe that this is an entirely modern city.

Behind the main thoroughfares, Collins Street, Bourke Street, there are small lanes, Little Collins Street, Little Bourke Street, that have an intimate quality and in the poorer districts there are whole terraces that might have been uprooted from the gaslight days of London, from Finsbury or Holloway.

19

KOOKABURRA BIRDS
Commonly known as the Laughing Jackass

It is at night that Melbourne is the most surprising: standing on the bridge that spans the Yarra, then Melbourne becomes every city in turn, there is a glimpse of London, Paris, Chicago.

Those pioneers had the Forsyte spirit. They believed in building solidly for the future. Soames Forsyte steps out of the Melbourne Club into the leafy shade of Collins Street a hundred times a day ; a hundred times from the comfort of his massive leather chair he grumbles that the country is going to the dogs. It must have taken courage to plant a St. James's Square Club in Batman's village and to wait for the village to grow into a city around it.

The homes, too (in the prosperous suburbs of Toorak, past St. Kilda, and elsewhere), are solid investments, beautifully built and beautifully kept.

Yes, perhaps the *cliché* is right after all and Melbourne is English, but neither the England of to-day nor the England of yesterday. An England as it would have developed free from continental entanglements. In climate, too, Melbourne is nearer to England, which may have helped to preserve the original character.

THE CUP CARNIVAL

Melbourne has its theatres and hotels, but there is little night-life and no cosmopolitanism apart from a few Italian restaurants and a handful of Chinese. Only one week in the year does Melbourne find room for frivolity and then it indulges in the carnival of Cup Week. The whole of Australia finds its way to Melbourne by plane, train, boat and road. And the racing is not like the Harrow and Eton match, an excuse for a top-hat and organdie party ; it is of interest to all, it compels a Bank holiday.

The Flemington race-course is but twenty minutes from the centre, it is not an exclusive function like Ascot, nor a hectic scramble like the Derby, but a tactful combination of the two. The lawns are ablaze with flowers, the Governor, top-hatted and accompanied by his suite, drives up, the band plays the anthem. The lawns are crowded with beautiful, magnificently but not extravagantly dressed women, the men, not so smartly dressed, throng the totalisator booths to back their fancy. It is easier to bet than not to bet, so splendidly is

20

THE FOUNDING OF AUSTRALIA

Oil painting by Algernon Talmadge

By courtesy of D. Hope Johnston, Esq.
and of the Medici Society

CAPTAIN COOK

Oil painting by Nathaniel Dance

this national institution organised.

Everybody seems to know everybody else and to share—until the race is over—the secret of form.

After the races come the cocktail-parties, after the cocktail-parties the dinner-parties, after the dinner-parties the balls at Government House, the Australian Club and elsewhere. For a week Melbourne goes gloriously mad and then settles down into its routine of hard work and home hospitality.

That, too, is the England of yesterday, of Swithin Forsyte, when

KOALA BEARS
A baby koala hanging on its mother's back

Derby Day meant an adjournment of Parliament, only in Australia the feast is more democratic and the sun shines.

THE ANIMALS NOAH FORGOT

Like Adelaide, Melbourne has its nearby playgrounds, though they take longer to reach through the shops, homes and cinemas that sprawl and straggle, Tooting-like, around.

The Dandenong ranges are rich in bird life and the primitive scenery that is Australia's alone. The animal sanctuary at Healesville is a sight that cannot be missed. There " the animals that Noah forgot " live with more freedom than in a Zoo, cared for by a curator, David Fleay, to whom they are individuals as well as specimens, from the noble wedge-tailed eagle, tame as a canary, to the meanest tiger-snake. Wenda, the wombat, muzzles against one like a dog and begs a biscuit for her tea; the kangaroos and wallabies gather around, giving an occasional kick to remind one of their presence. The star of the collection is that shy freak, the duck-billed platypus, a furry, semi-aquatic creature that lays eggs and suckles its young.

On the wires of a huge aviary the free parrots gather to chatter with the captives, a solid mass of scarlet.

They are all there at Healesville, even such a survival as the marsupial cat. It takes greater patience to see the animals at large, and luck as well.

The wallaby is frequent, picked up at night by the beams of the headlights; in wilder country the kangaroo and the emu can be seen. The possum shows his beady eyes like glow-worms in the trees at night, scrambles over the tin-roofs

21

CATTLE SWIMMING A FLOODED RIVER
Queensland

with a clatter that keeps many a countryman awake and cursing. The snake is frequent in certain districts and venomous, but fatal cases are a rarity. More often seen is the goanna, five foot six of lizard in thick and ill-fitting skin, rearing and clawing his way up a tree.

The greatest rarity, Australia's travel-poster pride, the Koala bear, can best be seen in his sanctuary, Phillip Island, a morning's journey from Melbourne. He is, apart from being something of a biological freak, a living teddy bear that arouses the maternal instincts in the most hard-boiled and, after slaughtering him in millions for a not very valuable fur, Australia has woken up to his value. He is featured in drawings, picture-postcards, toys and bags, until he has risen to the dignity of a creation by Walt Disney, as well he might be.

A TYPICAL AUSTRALIAN ENTERPRISE

It is not my intention here to give a history of the various colonies or of Australia itself, but now that we are in the great city of Melbourne, it is impossible to resist a hasty sketch of the founding of Victoria. It is perhaps the most inspiring in the whole history of Australia, differing in nearly every particular from the foundation of the other colonies, also, it is a typically Australian enterprise. As with the majority of British colonies, however, it

22

ONE OF THE LAST OF THE WINDJAMMERS
The *Pamir* off Sydney Heads

came as a natural growth, it was forced by the settlers themselves against the declared policy of the Government. In 1835, Melbourne was marked out in Batman's map as "a site reserved for a village"; sixteen years later Victoria was a flourishing and independent colony with 80,000 inhabitants, about a third of whom lived in the capital.

The eastern part of the coast of what was to become Victoria was first sighted in 1797 by George Bass in an open-boat expedition that altered the map of Australia by proving Van Diemen's Land to be an island. In 1802, Governor King sent Lieut. Murray, R.N., in the *Lady Nelson* to fill in some of the gaps left in the discoveries of Captain Grant. In January, 1802, he discovered a large harbour, which according to custom he named Port King, but King altered the name to that of his friend and patron, the first Governor and founder of Australia, Phillip.

"The southern shore of this noble harbour is bold highland in general, and not clothed, as all the land of Western Port is, with thick brush, but with stout trees of various kinds and in some places falls nothing short, in beauty and appearance, of Greenwick Park."

This enthusiastic report induced the Governor to form a settlement, a convict settlement, according to the usual policy. David Collins was put in command with wide discretionary powers. Unfortunately Collins was no Phillip. Although the Yarra had been surveyed Collins, with a sailor's instinct, clung to the sea shore. "As it was of the first consequence that the settlement should be of easy access to shipping, the shores near the mouth of the Port were first examined." The result was no fresh water.

Lieutenant Tuckey, who was with the expedition, writes in a prophetic vein: " . . . When I contrasted the powers, the ingenuity, and the resources of civilised man with the weakness, the ignorance, and the wants of the savage he came to dispossess, I acknowledged the immensity of human intelligence, and felt thankful for the small portion dispensed to myself. These thoughts naturally led to the contemplation of future possibilities. *I beheld a second Rome rising from a collection of banditti.*"

The convicts were accompanied by their wives and children and among them was an eleven-year-old London urchin, John Pascoe Fawkner. Thirty-two years later this urchin was to play a major role in the creation of that *second Rome.* Nor was he the only one in the party who was to share in the second chapter. John Buckley, a giant convict, escaped with some six others in a mad attempt to reach Sydney. The others failed, but Buckley disappeared into the bush where he emerges after thirty-two years and at the one moment of his life when he can be of service. With the failure of the Collins settlement all thoughts of occupying the Port Phillip district was abandoned for a considerable time. But where Governments are apathetic pastoralists seek new pastures for their drought-stricken sheep.

In 1815, Hamilton Hume, a bush-trained son by nature, and by instinct a born explorer, found new pastures in the Berrima district and a few years

24

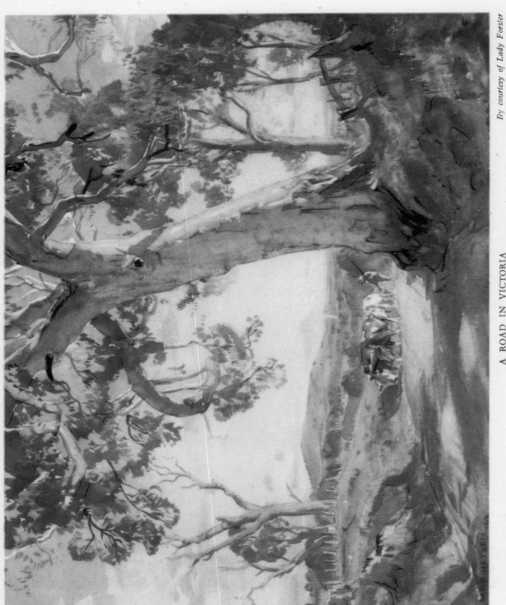

A ROAD IN VICTORIA

Water colour by Hans Heysen

By courtesy of
J. A. P. *Martin, Esq.*

LANDSCAPE AT OLINDA DANDENONG RANGE VICTORIA

Oil painting by Sir Arthur Streeton

later he discovered the Yass Plains, where to-day the finest wool is produced. The Government was sleeping, but the hungry sheep were closing in on the rich new district nibbling their way from the original settlement in every direction.

In 1824, Hume, in association with Alexander Hovell, made his most famous exploration under the auspices of Governor Brisbane, but at his own expense. No, that is not altogether fair. Government did assist to the tune of six pack saddles and gear, one tent of Parramatta cloth, two tarpaulins, a suit of slop clothes apiece, two skeleton charts upon which to trace a route and an order to Hume to select 1,200 acres, which order he subsequently had great difficulty in confirming! The Government was getting several millions of acres of new territory at a bargain price.

The explorers set out from Lake George with Spencer's Gulf as their objective. As we can now see from the map the route was practically impassable owing to the mountainous country. Only a great explorer could have overcome the unforeseen difficulties, and Hume was a very great explorer. On the 8th of November, the early Australian summer, he was rewarded by an extraordinary sight. Upon ascending a mountain to view the lay-out of the land he suddenly saw peak upon peak of snow-clad mountains, the Australian Alps, to-day the home of winter sports. But, unfortunately, his companion Hovell's calculation was wrong by one degree due east at the terminal point, making them think they had reached Western Port when they were near the present city of Geelong.

For many years the two explorers were bitterly antagonistic to one another, and a literature that need not concern us here has grown up around their unfortunate dispute. In spite of its mistake, which may have delayed the true settlement by a number of years, since their enthusiastic account could not be applied to the scrubby Western Port, the expedition was of capital value. The explorers passed a number of rivers—the Goulbourn, the Ovens, the Mitta Mitta and the Hume, which was actually a portion of the Murray (a river that should bear his name or that of Sturt, but certainly not that of an obscure minister), running west and north-west, which suggested that there must be an outlet into some great river and led to Sturt's epoch-making discovery of the Murray. Also, Hume's trail was later to become the principal route from Sydney to Melbourne and point the rich new pastures to shepherds and their hungry flocks.

In 1826 the usual alarm about French intentions, together with Hume's enthusiastic report, led Governor Darling to make a settlement at Western Port, which Hume had not visited, but this was abandoned two years later, when the French bogey had once again vanished into thin air.

John Batman, a schoolfellow of Hume's at Parramatta, and now a leading citizen of Launceston, had set his eyes on the mainland. His record showed him to be both fearless and ambitious. He had captured a number of bush-rangers, Jefferies, Hopkins, and the notorious but not altogether unchivalrous Matthew Brady single-handed. Batman is said to have come up to him in the mountains and called on him to surrender. " Are you an officer ? " asked

SHEEP ON SIR FREDERICK MCMASTER'S WELL-KNOWN STATION DALKEITH
New South Wales

Brady, coolly cocking his gun. "I'm not a soldier," replied Batman, "I'm John Batman. If you raise that gun I'll shoot. There's no chance for you." "You're right," replied Brady, "my time's come. You're a brave man and I yield; but I'd never have given in to a soldier."

His tact and humanity in assisting Governor Arthur in handling the unfortunate Tasmanian aborigines revealed another side to his character.

In 1827 this man of substance and ideas made an application to Governor Darling for the foundation of a settlement at Western Port.

"Sir—Understanding that it is your Excellency's intention to establish a permanent settlement at Western Port, and to afford encouragement to respectable persons to settle there, we beg leave most respectfully to solicit at the hands of your Excellency a grant of land at that place proportionable to the property which we intend to embark. We are in possession of some flocks of sheep highly improved, some of the Merino breed, and some of the pure South Devon; of some pure Devon cattle imported from England; and also of a fine breed of horses. We propose to ship from this place, 1,500 to 2,000 sheep, 30 head of superior cows, oxen, horses, etc., etc., to the value of from £4,000 to £5,000, the whole to be under the personal direction of Mr. Batman (who is a native of New South Wales), who will constantly reside there for the protection of the

26

establishment. Under these circumstances we are induced to hope your Excellency will be pleased to grant us a tract of land proportionable to the sum of money we propose to expend, and also to afford us every encouragement in carrying the proposed object into effect.

T. J. Gellibrand
John Batman

The Governor's minute of his reply to this important offer reads simply:

" Acknowledge and inform them that no determination having been come to with respect to the settlement of Western Port, it is not in my power to comply with their request.   March 17 (1827).—R.D."

MacArthur had created that land hunger. It took men of his breed and determination to satisfy it. Seldom did the council chamber have less to do with the building of a nation.

But such men did not understand a plain " No " for an answer when the land was there for the taking. At home in Downing Street an Australian square mile was taken to be the equivalent of an English square mile; a simple matter of mathematics. Surely these fellows had enough land already. Why should plain John Batman think in thousands of acres when at home a noble lord was happy with his hundreds? What was the need to extend our already large obligations, to police a whole new district many times the size of England? As long as the French did not interfere, we would do best to leave these lands to the few thousand aboriginals.

In March, 1836, a year after Batman's treaty of which we shall hear, Major Thomas Mitchell (afterwards Sir Thomas), Surveyor-General of New South Wales, an experienced explorer, set out under Government auspices to survey the Darling river. After discovering the Loddon and the Avoca, seduced by the richness and beauty of the country, his works prove him a true artist, he departed from his original plan and struck off to the S.W.

Homewards bound he discovered the Glenelg and on reaching Portland Bay found to his amazement that the Henty family had been established two years. The parties viewed one another with considerable suspicion, each one taking the other for a gang of escaped convicts. Major Mitchell was astonished by the only glass windows since he had left the boundary of New South Wales. From Mitchell, the Hentys learnt that the country 50 miles north was still more suitable and, as by now their sheep amounted to several thousand, they pushed on into the interior. They were the first.

But even before Mitchell had enhanced its value by discovering the interior wealth, the stubborn Batman was not to be put off from his plan of settling Port Phillip. If the Government would not help, he was prepared to act on his own. He was further encouraged by the results of Sturt's explorations. South Australia was about to be founded, the Hentys had settled in their promised land. Delay was intolerable.

He determined to go to Port Phillip and make his own arrangement with the natives. At Merri Creek, in 1835, he signed his famous, but unrecognised treaty with the natives, by which Jaga Jaga and others, " do for ourselves, our heirs, and successors, give, grant, enfeoff and confirm unto the said John Batman, etc., etc." All very correct, but not very informative to Jaga Jaga and others.

At about this point the long lost Buckley arrives upon the scene after living as an aboriginal and with the aboriginals for thirty-two years. He came at an opportune moment to act as interpreter. He was a singularly stupid man, who strays into history as a footnote.

Meanwhile, the third actor, a one time convict's brat, John Pascoe Fawkner, had also come over with a party from Launceston to occupy the territory and had invaded part of Batman's preserves. These extraordinary men were contending for a district that Government had no intention of settling.

A compromise was finally reached between Batman, Fawkner and the Government, and from that moment Tuckey's *New Rome* sprang up almost over night. Behind it was the rich pasture land of Mitchell's *Australia Felix*.

Batman died young, Fawkner lived to a great age, a power for progress in Melbourne.

This is a hurried and, because abbreviated, a not wholly accurate picture of a very involved chapter of history. I have avoided a close study of the chronology which is important. My sole object here is to show the extraordinary private enterprise of the British in Australia that could by confronting the Government with a *fait accompli*, add vast new wealth to the Empire without the shedding of a drop of blood. A typically British enterprise.

BUSH FIRES

Victoria is the smallest state, but its pasture-lands are rich in feed, its climate less given to extremes, though like all Australia it is a prey to drought and bush fire. And how terrible those bush fires can be, springing up in an instant, borne with a crackle, a rush and a roar along the tops of the trees, outpacing the fastest horse, then swooping into some peaceful valley destroying bush and homestead as they pass. For days they rage until some fortunate combination of wind and rain, aided by the courage and skill of the bushman stifles and extinguishes them. They fill the air with pungent smoke, stifle nearby cities with their heat, the birds hover and fall into the furnace. And where they have passed nothing remains but a fine black powder. What were giant trees still stand, but so brittle that a gentle breeze would send them tumbling.

But nature is kinder than man in repairing her destruction. A day or two of rain and green shoots poke their way out of the charcoal. The scene is still one of devastation, but it bears the promise of life and strength. The ants and the birds return and the settler rebuilds his homestead.

MARCH OF THE GHOSTS

Fortunately such major disasters as the great fires of the drought year of 1939 are rare and measures have been taken to make them rarer still.

Have the present-day pastoralists in so blessed a district lost the drive of their fathers? That is a natural question to ask. They have greater leisure and security, but the essential struggle with the land remains. They have the aid of science in dealing with their problems; they are mechanised, but still the same in spirit and outlook. The slacker may have more rope, but he will go under in the end. The gifts needed for this pastoral life are many. The character and ability to handle men, a knowledge of biology, chemistry and finance. The ability to forestall the weather. They may dance in Melbourne, visit the race-track and the theatre; at home they enjoy all the comforts of modern plumbing, but just the same they must ride as hard and work as hard as the men they employ.

MELBOURNE TO SYDNEY : CANBERRA

There are many alternative routes from Melbourne to Sydney. The train is luxuriously comfortable until Albury on the New South Wales border, where it is necessary to change owing to the narrowing of the gauge, a survival of the lack of co-operation between states. The interstate boats, large vessels of 12,000 tons, are deservedly popular in summer. The most attractive routes of all are by the two famous roads, the Prince's Highway and the Hume Highway.

The Prince's Highway runs along the coast, past chains of lakes that join the sea, past the small townships that have become famous as the centres of big

FEDERAL PARLIAMENT HOUSE CANBERRA
New South Wales

game fishing, past the richest oyster-bearing beds on a continent where oysters are a penny a piece. It is a memorable drive and it is the one that the Australian always recommends to the foreigner, a four-day Amalfi to Sorrento. It is, however, the Hume Highway, the inner road, that is the most characteristically Australian in scenery. Mile upon mile of undulating plain, covered with a dried, yellowing vegetation that produces the finest of all wool. Forests of dead trees stick out of the ground, ringbarked by man, fired or lightning struck. Small homesteads with the inevitable round water tanks elevated on stilts can be seen miles away by the flash of the sun on their corrugated surface. It is not a happy or smiling landscape, there is no hint of prettiness, but it is beautiful in a way that words cannot describe. It belongs to another planet. It is on the Hume Highway that one will love or loathe Australia. And, if one loves it, no other landscape can ever give just that feeling of inner peace and detachment, a feeling of distance, space and sanity.

Between Melbourne and Sydney, but nearer to Sydney, lies the capital of the Australian Federation—Canberra. Canberra is the artificial result of the disagreement of two cities. It is unfinished and has not the meaning of the smallest township nearby that seems to have grown out of its surroundings. Canberra is beautiful, artificially so, when the millions of ornamental trees and shrubs arranged with geometrical precision are in blossom. It is situated in the most perfect of natural surroundings, some 2,000 feet above sea level, an amphitheatre in the middle of a group of hills. Its buildings have the dignity of the administrative offices of some huge exhibition and Canberra is still an exhibition, waiting to be assimilated into the life and atmosphere of Australia. More attractive by far is the little Federal Port of Jervis Bay, insignificant by comparison, a seaside township with all the charm of a Portofino. In Canberra the tourist will be interested in statistics, at Jervis Bay he will relax.

ARTHUR PHILLIP FOUNDER OF SYDNEY 1788
Oil painting by Francis Wheatley

NEW SOUTH WALES

IN Sydney lies the beginning of the history of Australia, and Sydney should be called Phillip in memory of its founder, one of the greatest and least known figures in British history. Botany Bay was the original destination of that First Fleet. The continent of Australia was an unknown quantity.

The only guidance that the pioneers possessed was from the account of the brief stay by Cook and especially Banks, the first men who had set foot on the eastern shores of Australia. Phillip had wanted to sail ahead of the transports to explore and prepare the terrain, but his plan had not been accepted and he was only able to arrive two days ahead. His instructions called for haste. They left him a choice, but told him to hurry.

In that short time he had a decision to make affecting the whole future of the colony. An unhealthy exposed situation, resulting in a high death rate and the plan would have been written off another failure, leaving Australia to the French, a distinct possibility and one of the many interesting historical *ifs*.

Here is Phillip's own simple account of the great decision, in a dispatch to Lord Sydney, dated from Sydney Cove, May 15th, 1788.

" The 25th, being eighty leagues to the eastward of the Cape, I left *Sirius* and went on board the *Supply*, tender, in hopes, by leaving the convoy, to gain sufficient time to examine the country round Botany Bay, and fix on the most eligible situation for the colony before the transports arrived.

" The westerly winds we now had continued till the 3rd of January, when we saw the coast of New South Wales, but the winds which had been so favourable, having seldom been to the eastward, and then for a few hours only, blowing to the N.W. from the S.W., generally very strong gales, now left us, and we had variable winds, with a current that at times set very strong to the southward, so that we did not arrive at Botany Bay before the 18th.

" The *Alexander*, *Scarborough* and *Friendship* came in the next day, and the *Sirius*, with the rest of the ships, the day after. Those ships had continued very healthy.

LANDSCAPE NEAR CANBERRA NEW SOUTH WALES   *By courtesy of J. A. P. Martin, Esq.*

Water colour by Harold Herbert

SCENE ON AN AUSTRALIAN FARM

Oil painting by Sir Arthur Streeton

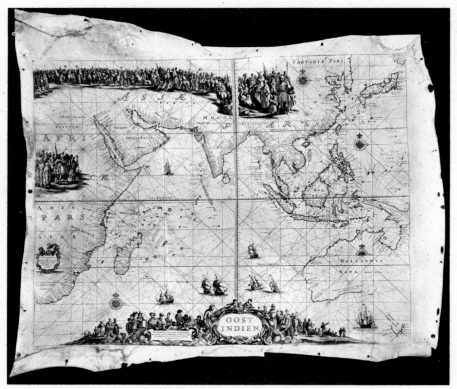

PRINTED PORTULON BY PETER GOOS
The kind of map Captain Cook would have used

" The *Supply*, sailing very badly, had not permitted my gaining the advantage hoped for, but I began to examine the bay as soon as we anchored, and found that, tho' extensive, it did not afford shelter to ships from the easterly winds; the greater part of the bay being so shoal that ships of even a moderate draught of water are obliged to anchor with the entrance of the bay open, and are exposed to a heavy sea that rolls in when it blows hard from the eastward.

" Several small runs of fresh water were found in different parts of the bay, but I did not see any situation to which there was not some very strong objection."

" Several good situations offered from a small number of people, but none that appeared calculated for our numbers, and where the stores and provisions could be landed without a great loss of time. When I considered the Bay's being so very open, and the probability of the swamps rendering the most eligible situation unhealthy, I judged it advisable to examine Port Jackson;

but that no time might be lost if I did not succeed in finding a better harbour, and a proper situation for the settlement, the ground near Point Sutherland was in the meantime to be cleared and preparations made for landing under the direction of the Lieutenant-Governor.

" As the time in which I might be absent, if I went to the *Supply*, must have been very uncertain, I went round with three boats, taking with me Captain Hunter and several officers, that by examining different parts of the port at the same time less time might be lost.

" We got into Port Jackson early in the afternoon, and had the satisfaction of finding *the finest harbour in the world, in which a thousand sail of the line may ride in the most perfect security.*

" The different coves were examined with all possible expedition. I fixed on the one that had the best spring of water, and in which the ships can anchor so close to the shore that at a very small expense quays may be made at which the largest ships may unload.

" This cove, which I honoured with the name of Sydney, is about a quarter of a mile across at the entrance, and half a mile in length."

This is a very matter of fact announcement of a great achievement, how great neither Phillip nor Sydney were to live to see. Those lines, " *the finest harbour in the world, in which a thousand sail of the line may ride in the most perfect security,*" remove the enterprise from the sordid association of Botany Bay, by which it was so long to be called. They mark the beginning of a history as glorious as any in our annals, we must remember them when stupidity, cupidity and petty quarrels obscure that fact, when, in the subsequent history of Australia, Botany Bay and Sydney Cove or " finest harbour in the world," are fighting for supremacy.

The cove should, of course, have been named Phillip.

THE CONVICT BOGEY

A point that must be dealt with here might be called the convict bogey. The First Fleet, eleven ships of a total tonnage of 3,892, was a fleet of convicts and their guardians; " Botany Bay " was founded to rid England of her criminals, and the fact that Australia subsequently became a Dominion was due to an accident, but mainly to the qualities of those who had become Australians. Those are the bare facts. When Australia was founded the American colonies had been recently lost. Not even Pitt himself foresaw that Australia might make good the loss.

For a long time the colony was known as Botany Bay, and those words had the same significance as Newgate. It is important, however, to remember that the convicts of those days were by no means all criminals. A high pro-

THE JAMIESSON VALLEY IN THE BLUE MOUNTAINS
New South Wales

portion were men of exceptional intelligence and courage, who had been leaders in new movements, like the men from the Dorset village of Tolpuddle who started the first agricultural trade union.   To-day only about 1 per cent. of the Australians are descended from the convicts, and the story of the nation's origin has a purely psychological interest.   The change in the status of the colony came about through the influx of free settlers and through the fact that the land gave opportunities to the emancipists and their children that they would not have had at home. Fawkner of Melbourne is an outstanding example.   The experiment was attended by suffering and cruelty, the age was a callous one at home as well, but it was essentially a success.

The glorious lesson to be learned from it, an example to the modern world, is that a nation, begun in cruelty, oppression and chaos, could within a short period become a model of ordered democracy, the home and the champion of freedom.   That is the inspiring message of Australian history, a history of systematic progress without the battles that have scarred the story of other nations, however glorious the single episodes.   Australia shows the Anglo-Saxon genius for democratic government.

35

BULLOCK TEAM
Even now a widely used method of transport

THE OLD SYDNEY

Sydney saw the emergence of a remarkable man, John Macarthur, the first to introduce the Merino into Australia and alter the whole meaning of that continent. It saw his struggle for power with three Governors, his deposition of the much maligned Bligh of *Bounty* fame. His dogged determination to enrich himself enriched Australia. Sydney was the scene of that great struggle of adolescence between the emancipist and the free settler, a passionate but bloodless civil war in which Charles Wentworth was the first Australian to speak for Australia. In its names and buildings it is still closely linked with the great Governor of that period, Lachlan Maquarie, the benevolent despot with a passion for building. During his rule, with the penetration of the Blue Mountains that had cut Sydney off from the interior, a settlement became a nation. That is a part of the fascination of Sydney. It grew up in haphazard fashion, bullock tracks became tramlines as it sprawled its way around the finest harbour in the world.

THE NEW SYDNEY

The old Sydney still lives on in the mists of evening. The new Sydney is very different, a city of sunshine and laughter. That, at any rate, is how it strikes the visitor who sips his cocktail at the " Australia," plays golf at Rose Bay and bathes at Palm Beach. There is work in Sydney as in Melbourne, but

36

THE FAMOUS BRIDGE
Sydney Harbour

to the visitor—and I am writing here from the visitor's point of view—it is as much a Riviera resort as Nice or Miami. He is not allowed to be conscious of the fact that Sydney exists for anything but his own pleasure.

Sydney has a restaurant life and a night life. Its large hotel, the *Australia*, is the casino of its pleasure-resort aspect. Everyone drops in to pass the time of day and the atmosphere is always one of excitement, the atmosphere that Melbourne reserves for one week in the year. In truth there are many other Sydneys than the old or the frivolous ; there are as many Sydneys as there are inlets to its vast harbours. It is a capital and a fishing village, a busy port and a place to lounge in. It seems to reveal itself immediately and it goes on showing new and unsuspected angles. It is one of the most fascinating cities in the world.

Up in King's Cross there is a city within a city, a Montmartre, Chelsea, Greenwich village, where artists, theatricals, would-be artists and would-be theatricals, but chiefly very ordinary birds of passage congregate. For a time they can be inhabitants of Sydney and set up housekeeping in a modern flat rented by the week or month, and housekeeping is easy, for the fruiterers and delicatessen shops are always open and always tempting.

Sydney is ringed by magnificent surfing beaches where most of the population burns itself brown. There are sharks off the coast, but who cares ! Only the newcomer who has seen the menacing pig-eyed beasts cruising in the Taronga Park aquarium and who is not soothed by statistics treads delicately at first. The currents can be treacherous and the waves high, but there are life-savers to deal with that, corps of young men, perfect swimmers, trained to the minute, on the constant look-out to rescue and revive the unwary. They are a magnificent sight. Their discipline is perfect.

Australian discipline has often been questioned, the surf clubs provide the answer. It is the discipline of the man confronted by a sudden danger, the discipline of the man who thinks things out for himself, the pioneer, the bushman. The Australian does not recognise discipline for the sake of discipline. To be disciplined in battle is one thing, a little laxity in saluting is another. To watch these surf club members at work is a revelation.

A source of considerable pride is " our bridge," an imposing steel structure that spans the harbour. Certainly it is a marvel of engineering ; certainly it is essential to speed and comfort in circulation ; but in beauty it can add nothing to " the finest harbour in the world " and at times it detracts. Only at night when it is a weightless arc of lights does it truly belong there.

As in the other cities Sydney has its pleasure grounds, near at hand Taronga Park Zoo, Koala Park at Pennant Hills and a vast portion of tamed bush, the National Park. Further south, the Bulli pass at Sublime Point presents a breath-taking view of beaches and pounding surf.

The main excursion is to the Blue Mountains, the barrier that imprisoned the tiny settlement for so many years. To-day a stream of cars and buses follow the route of the original pioneers, Wentworth, Blaxland and Lawson,

IN THE BLUE MOUNTAINS
New South Wales

" who changed the aspect of the colony, from a confined insulated tract of land, to a rich and extensive continent." From Katoomba the view down below into the Jameson valley is grandiose, a sheer precipitous drop into a bowl of trees and ferns, and on the other side another steep rise into mountains that are constantly changing colour from deep blue to grey. When the valley fills with mists, the trees are submerged under a mystic lake of bottomless depth that seems to be fed by the falls that trickle or rush down the cliff face. With every few paces the view changes, now serene, now dramatic.

And beyond the Blue Mountains are the fertile plains of Bathurst, townships and stations that feed the cities.

YOUNG ABORIGINES PLAYING ROUND A BARK SHELTER
Queensland

QUEENSLAND

BRISBANE: GATEWAY TO THE TROPICS

Each of the capital cities differs widely in atmosphere and aspect, that is the charm of Australian travel, but Brisbane differs most of all. Like Perth it is most cut off from the other states and retains a feeling of pioneering. There is a heightening of colour and humidity, a feeling that this is the gateway to the tropics. Again there is the dignified Municipal core, the 20th century city, but the suburbs surrounding it are more picturesque to European eyes with their houses, largely made of wood, propped up on stilts. And the streets are a mass of blossom, poiciana, poinsetia, bougainvillea, cascara, casting shadows from the palette of a Renoir. The city area is immense, winding round the S-bend of the Brisbane river and gradually petering out in a rough bushlike countryside.

The topee is seen in the streets and, unlike the rest of the seaboard, men remember that they live in a hot climate and wear light semi-tropical clothes.

ABORIGINAL SPEARING FISH
North Queensland

There is no pretence in playing at London here. The physique of the men also has undergone a change. They are tall, lean, loose-limbed, hatchet-faced, bronzed. The heat seems to have fired them instead of softening. Brisbane is more energetic than Sydney. Like Perth its frontiers stretch into the tropical jungle where the aboriginal is still a savage and its cattle stations run into thousands of square miles where men know loneliness and danger.

I have concentrated here on the cities, where the mass of the population lives, but it is the solitude that justifies and keeps those cities alive. And unlike the rest of the world the aeroplane and the wireless have proved a blessing and have lived up to their inventors' aspirations. An axe slips, maiming its wielder, a hasty call on the wireless and the " flying doctor " is on his way with help. A valuable life is saved where yesterday the victim would have bled to death. The " flying doctor " and his service is opening up the interior, making it possible for women and children to live there, in hardship still, but in greater security. He is playing his part in the solution of Australia's problem of population. For once modern science has not been misapplied.

Brisbane and its surroundings are but a fragment of Queensland, potentially the richest of states, but that fraction contains samples of the whole. There are farms that grow a variety of tropical fruit, paw-paws, bananas, pineapples, alligator pears and mangos. All of which should not be taken for granted. When Phillip landed with his small party, Australia did not produce enough food to save them from famine, and when the transports from home were delayed, twice they were faced with complete annihilation.

The aboriginals lived on a diet of kangaroo, grubs, snakes, goannas. Tilling or stock-breeding was unknown and there were none of the riches of the South Sea Islands that come without work. Every sheep, every cow, every apple, every pear, every banana, sugar, wheat, maize—the list is inexhaustible—all have been brought in by the settler and developed by him. The climate can produce everything, the land had nothing.

Man has not always imported so wisely. The rabbit, notorious in Australia, is a case in point. Imported originally for food, perhaps also as a nostalgic reminder of home, it has overrun the country. Where to-day the dreaded convict is but a memory, bunny is a menace, causing erosion and robbing the flocks of much-needed pasture. The fox, too, has caused damage to the native fauna, hunting the most wonderful of all birds, the mimic lyre-bird, destroying the koala. So that just as socially Australia started with a clean slate, it did agriculturally.

North from Brisbane begins a new tour of Australia, without cities, milk bars, cinemas and Woolworths, without the little houses and trim gardens, the white wicker prams and the tamed pleasure-park bush.

TASMANIA

I HAVE left Tasmania last on my tour; geographically it belongs to Melbourne which its settlers founded. It is cut off from Melbourne by a turbulent mass of water, the Bass Straits. The aeroplane has made it a casual excursion.

Tasmania goes its own pace, unaffected by the modernity of Melbourne and Sydney. It is a survival of yesterday's Australia, closely related to the old country. In its settled districts it has the serenity of cosiness denied to the mainland. The word *farm* seems more applicable than the Australian *station*. Man has planted English trees which contest the landscape with the native gum, and the apple orchards have more than a suggestion of Devon. There are little churches too, dotted about the countryside, that bring a sharp reminder of home. A coach rattling along the road would not seem an anachronism.

Yet this peaceful countryside has witnessed the most turbulent scenes, and the early settler had to lay out his land with his gun by his side to guard against the bands of bushrangers that threatened all security. Tasmania was made a penal settlement within a penal settlement and was in use after the other colonies had successfully revolted. To-day the bush has grown over the ruins of those cruel days, effacing the memory. Port Arthur, stronghold of the system, is a deserted village, centre of interest for the charabanc tourist and the historian. It is good to gaze (there in the most peaceful spot on earth) upon this bracken-covered home of totalitarianism, to see the cells with their broken

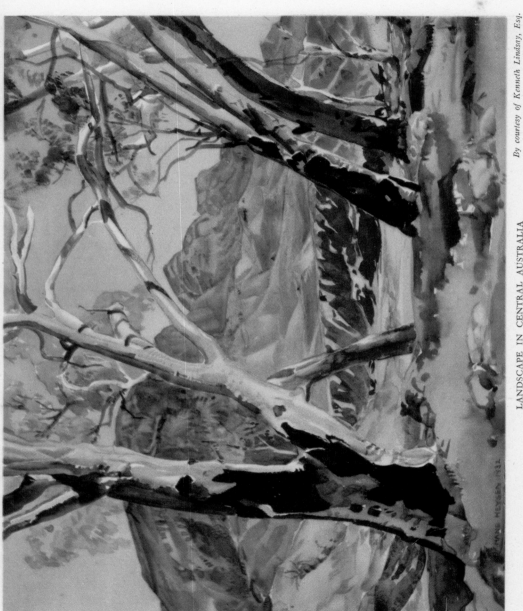

By courtesy of Kenneth Lindsay, Esq.

LANDSCAPE IN CENTRAL AUSTRALIA

Water colour by Hans Heysen

LANDSCAPE AT MICHELAGO NEW SOUTH WALES

Oil painting by George Lambert

bars and the fallen masonry that lets in the light of the sun. It is good to know that man has willed this curse away.

Hobart, the capital, is situated beneath Mount Wellington on the finest and deepest harbour in the world, Sydney included. It is first cousin to a small English cathedral city; Launceston, the southern city, a country town. Their old-world atmosphere is only dispelled at night when the neon lights give them an air of false gaiety. There is no night life behind the lights. Carefully hidden, too, beneath the old-world atmosphere is the commercial wealth of woollen, zinc and other factory work.

Tasmania understands the tourist problem and "Tassy," as it is affectionately called, is a favourite holiday resort for those of the mainland. The foreign tourist has yet to learn the way to Tasmania. It is the one part of Australia certain to please the Englishman

THE RUSSELL FALLS IN THE NATIONAL PARK
Tasmania

who has a natural sympathy for islands. There is fishing in plenty in the Great Lakes, the type that has made New Zealand and Scotland a sportsman's paradise. The climate, too, is closer to our own, though the sunshine exceeds anything in these islands.

THE POLITICAL CONSTITUTION

AUSTRALIA consists of six separate States, each with a parliament consisting of two Houses. At the head of each State is a Governor, who used always to be sent out from England to represent the King, so that the parliament of each State was a model of the British parliament and the Governor had the same constitutional role to play in each State as the King in Great Britain. On January 1st, 1901, the States, which until then had been Colonies quite independent of each other, united, and formed the federal Commonwealth of Australia with a Governor-General and a federal parliament, consisting of two Houses—a Senate and a House of Representatives. The legislature consists of the King, represented by the Governor-General, the Senate and the House of Representatives. In the Senate the equality of States is recognised, each having six representatives irrespective of population, in the House members are elected in proportion to State population. The State legislatures exercise powers not mentioned in the constitution as federal. They control public lands and works, justice (apart from federal questions), inter-state trade, railways, education, etc.

The Australians have tackled the problems of native administration with skill and success, though in the early days of settlement there was much suffering and harsh suppression of the native tribes. The modern Australian practice is in the forefront of intelligent administration : when trouble broke out in the Northern Territory, one of Australia's leading anthropologists was sent to live in the district, make friends with the natives and gain their confidence ; this he succeeded in doing, and the new administrative system, based partly on old tribal customs, works to the satisfaction of all parties.

The Commonwealth of Australia, like the other great Dominions of the British Commonwealth of Nations, is an entirely self-governing and independent sovereign state ; appoints its own representatives abroad and administers its own mandate in New Guinea. This independence, which had been a matter of fact for many years, was established by law after the war of 1914–1918 by the celebrated Statute of Westminster, which put the independence of the Dominions on a constitutional footing.

Thus Australia is left entirely free to intervene on the side of England or to remain neutral. She is free to appoint ministers to other nations. Her freedom is very real.

The bond between the Commonwealth of Australia and Great Britain or any of the Dominions, is thus almost entirely one of sentiment and tradition. The Governor-General, however, is appointed by the British Government, as also the State governors ; both the King and his representative have the right of veto ; appeals may be made from the High Court to the Privy Council ; and

CUTTING ENSILAGE ON A FARM
New South Wales

Australian parliaments cannot annex territory without power from the Crown.
In spite of these reservations, the first remark holds good and the link is one of
sentiment, tradition and of a common king.

Actually the population of Australia is about 98–99 per cent. British, but
this in no way diminishes their feeling of independence. It is all the more
significant, therefore, that both in 1914 and in 1939, the Australian Government
with the backing of the whole people, immediately and without hesitation
declared war on Germany.

SOCIAL LIFE AND THE ARTS

MOST writers on Australia have stressed the discomfort of the never-never
at the expense of the life lived by the vast majority of Australians and have
created a totally wrong impression. There are pioneers in Australia, but the
country as a whole has passed the pioneer stage and must be written of in the
same manner as England or America. Australia is a land of surprises and the
greatest surprise of all, after the vast quantity of negative writing that exists,
is the high degree of comfort to be found in every settled district. The homes
of the well-to-do are more modern in style than anything to be found in this

country and the artisan is correspondingly better off. The gardens, both large and small, are cared for with skill, and the flower arrangements to be seen in most homes show an extraordinary degree of art. Flowers play a large part in Australian life. There are some unjustified slums in Australian cities, but there is no actual starvation in the European sense of the word. Australia has its wealthy men, but there are none of the great extremes of the United States. Labour, as apart from Marxist socialism, has a strong voice in affairs, the labour of the individualist. Masses are not easily dragooned in a pioneer country. The working man has a guaranteed wage, graduated according to the scale of living and periodically revised by a Court of Conciliation and Arbitration.

Socially Australia is still more democratic. There are no hereditary titles, there is a minimum of snobbery; a man must prove his own worth and the quality most appreciated is that of good fellowship. America prides itself on its democracy, Australia, less given to self-dramatisation, takes it for granted. The Australian does not know the politeness of servility. He is exceptionally polite, because he is exceptionally goodhearted. If you can carry your bag, then carry it, but, if it appears a load, he will be the first to volunteer. His attitude to the visitor is especially pleasing, it is one of interest. He has the quality of a superb listener. He is only arrogant when challenged, the arrogance of self-defence.

The hotels in the large capitals are like hotels everywhere. It is in the smaller hotels and guest houses that a truer picture can be gained. The table is good in basic materials, varied in that it swings between beef, lamb, turkey and pork, but cooked without much imagination. Tea is the universal drink. The climate tends to make lounges stuffy, but life is lived largely on the verandahs that surround the house. In the summer, life in a guest house is largely one of camping, with very little privacy. The sanitary arrangements vary according to the quantity of water in the district. At the worst they are primitive but not unhygienic. Service is cheerful, willing, scanty. It is surprising how one has grown used to being over-serviced.

The Australian enjoys considerable leisure. How does he spend it? Largely in sport.

The Australian is a born sportsman and sport in Australia is within the reach of all. The certainty of fine weather gives him added hours of tennis, golf and cricket. Cricket has an importance unknown in this country. Bradman a position far above that of the popular athlete. He represents an important aspect of Australian life. The Australian can surf in the sea, yacht in the harbours, fish in the sea and the rivers, and bake in the sun on the warm sand. Riding is as much a necessity as a sport. Mountain châlets in Victoria, New South Wales and Tasmania provide winter sports and at a price impossible in Europe. It is said that the Australian cares for his body at the expense of his mind. There is some element of truth in that. Mentally he inclines to indolence and an easy tolerance that could make him the prey of some political adventurer. Yet he would react violently were his liberties too

46

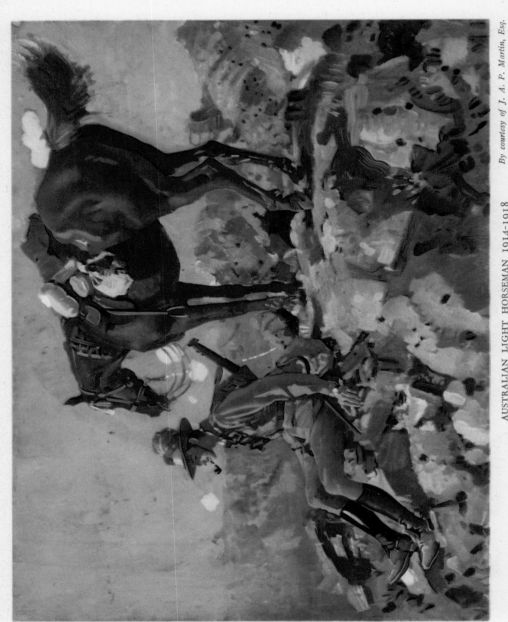

AUSTRALIAN LIGHT HORSEMAN 1914-1918

Oil painting by George Lambert

By courtesy of Lady Forster

GUM TREES

Water colour by Hans Heysen